I0192111

Was It R*pe

Elisabeth Horan

Copyright © 2021 Elisabeth Horan

All Rights Reserved. This book or any portion thereof may not be reproduced, in whole or in part, in any form (beyond that permitted by Sections 107 and 108 of the U.S Copyright Law and except by reviewers for the public press), without the express written permission of the publisher except for the use of brief quotations in a book review.

Horan / Elisabeth, author

Was It R*pe / Elisabeth Horan

Poems

ISBN: 978-1-7365167-2-0

Book Design: Tianna G. Hansen & Amanda McLeod
Cover Art: Elisabeth Horan
Cover Design: Amanda McLeod

Fémme Salvé
Books

An Imprint of Animal Heart Press

PUBLISHER
Femme Salvé Books
An Imprint of Animal Heart Press
P.O. Box 322
Thetford Center, Vermont 05075
www.femmesalvebooks.net

Content Warning: This work deals heavily with sexual assault and its aftermath of trauma. Please take extra care while reading.

Advance Praise for *Was It R*pe*

"The poetry in this collection by Elisabeth Horan is brimming with pain and power. This is the voice of a poet who is fighting back – the voice of a poet who isn't giving up. These poems sting, burn, scratch and tear. And yet they are beautiful. And yet there is hope."

~ Cathy Ulrich,
founding editor, Milk Candy Review

"What constitutes rape? What does it take for others to believe survivors of sexual assault, to support them, to give them justice they deserve? Elisabeth Horan looks at us readers dead in the eye and asks sincerely, 'Is it rape if no one hears / you, is it rape if he didn't kill you.' Horan already knows the answer, so do we feel it, but when will everyone else? What does it take to be believed? *Was it R*pe* is a collection of raw and bold poems that asks such hard questions unabashedly with fire, stings, and fury. It's a twisting and turning journey all too familiar, all too painful, from that of a survivor to that of someone who has survived. 'I don't want to play anymore – / no sunshine day charades.' Horan writes, encouraging herself, ourselves, our humanity, to feel the anger fully, to accept it as valid, to be real with it. Because yes, it happened, and we're entitled to feel furious and to get the justice we deserve."

~ Nadia Gerassimenko,
founding editor, Moonchild Mag

"Elisabeth Horan makes no apologies in this collection, starting off with the visceral first poem, CW: 'triggered / this warning – means nothing / these knees – worn to bone from kneeling'. From there we weave deeper into sexual assault, the #MeToo movement, and the expectations put on young women. Horan does an excellent job pulling the reader in and allowing them to live in the poem. In   , was his name she expertly uses blank spaces to allow the reader to fill them in as they see fit; it simultaneously creates and fills a hole in the reader. This collection of poems isn't always easy to read but that is why it's so very necessary, Horan gives a voice to women everywhere and allows us to feel less alone. In these poems we see ourselves and we see others."

~ Courtney LeBlanc,
author of *Beautiful & Full of Monsters* (Vegetarian Alcoholic Press)

Dear Reader –

Thank you for holding this book in your hands. I appreciate you taking the chance to read my words.

Silence is something we succumb to when we have been told that the consequences for sharing are worse than what happened to us. At least that is how I felt 30 years ago when I told the police I had been sexually assaulted. I left the station ashamed, afraid and alone, embarking on a path of self-hatred and self-destruction which remains a part of me even today. I was so embarrassed, that I had been violated in such a way, a way which left me ashamed of myself, of my body, of my soul, that I tried for all those years to kill myself slowly, ever-kindling the slow burn of self-hate – yet all the while, trying so hard to make others love me, when there was only emptiness inside to love.

September, 2018: I watched in horror as Christine Blasey Ford testified in front of our country. I watched, not in disbelief, as she was asked to replay all of the unspeakable memories for the Court, and I felt the tears burning, my hands shaking, as if I already knew the outcome... with his rebuttal that it was a witch hunt, a circus, a democratic ploy to ruin the lives of good men... and watched our highest court believe... him. But what about the lives of women? What about my life? Our lives? Am I therefore the circus? The witch hunt... is it all a ploy of the patriarchy to tear me down and silence me? Us? Is this the survivor's cross to bear?

I took action that week, and I wrote this book. I wrote it as Ford gave her testimony; I recalled the laughter of men in my ears, even while despicable things happened to me as a young teen. I recalled the stinging tears, the shame, the terror of going to school, my inability to live in the world.
To ever be 'normal' again. To feel like 'damaged goods'.

This is my story. This is my testimony. I am still afraid to tell it. I'd be lying if I said otherwise. But what I do feel is the support of millions of women, who have felt the stinging tears, the disbelief, the persecution. This is my contribution of support to those who have told their stories, and those not yet able to. To Blasey Ford. To all of us. May we hold each other up in love and solidarity.

I believe you, and I love you. No more silence.

Eli

Was It R*pe

for us

CW

We are Women

triggered
this warning – means nothing
these knees – worn to bone from kneeling

doubled over I place my hands on the floor, exhausting
my survival skills are waning
lovely bones are what we keep becoming

in the DOJ, on the Floor of the Senate
in the boarded up houses – at least we r anonymous
in those abandoned places; we hang ribbons on trees
and in the windows, whispering: Stop looking at us

we are not our rapists' sneers and smiles –
nor are we a drinking game – (can you tell which frat boy
held her down); nor pawns in the endless patriarchal chess game.

we bear children, smiles, surgeries,
the weight of each others' pain;
no longer shall we live as trigger warnings;
no longer do we warn these men---

look out – we are coming for you (   )
we are coming out as loaded guns; retaliating

these knees – worn to bone from kneeling
this warning – means nothing
triggered

We are Women

CW

Was It R*pe ---

he did this, I know, a penetration... No
insertion, but some kind of, tongue and lips
and oh God, so vile, did I want it, did I ask
did my hips betray my mind, did the drink
ing earn the crime, did young blushing
cheeks belie a want, perversion, deserve
the panties down, around the ankles, a
betrayal ground. Is it rape if no one hears
you, is it rape if he didn't kill you. Is it rap
e, unprosecuted, is it legitimate pain if he
did not impregnate you. Is this real if I w
rite about it, if no one reads it, or tweets
about it. Am I a victim or a liar. Am I a g
irl who asked for it. Am I a woman bur
ning in pain – a slave, forever fuckin-slut-sham
ed?

or am I on fire ---

Doing Nothing at a Party (While a Drunk Girl Gets Destroyed By a Sex Predator)

An open letter to the "_____ " of _____ High School, class of 19__

I can't be quieter,
more passive than this
for nothing can be the greater sin

Than not standing up and stepping in
when a young woman is having her life
raped out from within her
as you pretend not to listen –

When you left the room, did you think he was planning
to hold her, stroke her softly –
kiss her cheek like a lover: protectively?

That he'd only take a peek at her pert little chest
and not go so far overboard, like
the rest of the world knew he would?

Did you know when she passed out, it was
you she was groping for;
hoping for
her sweet-lipped-baby-hued-kiss
meant for
you you you

But you didn't want her. (Ok, I get it.
That pain still bruises me black and blue
right in the eye
like that cigarette where you branded me -
another letter, another day).

There could have been a better way,
a more humane way, to make her see
what could have been
than stand by as a different man
violates her body and breaks her so violently
she still hasn't found all the pieces so many years later
from the wreck around her on

The wretched floor

which doesn't ever fall away
no matter how hard she yells at it –
(why will it not just give up
and drop away beneath her seismic feet?)

Give this woman her chance with bliss
after all the years years years
of therapy
(you have no idea)

All because you didn't *feel* like it
didn't feel like speaking up as you lingered idly by,
your fingers hovering over the handle
(you understand me)

Just know, I've seen how
doing nothing can destroy someone.

Something. That's what you could have
done, but did not do.

You made your choices –
so quietly; so passively.

Death Wish

*All in all you're just another
brick in the wall*

When I was 16
Two tabs under/over
Glass rained over
Me, the shotgun
On the table
The goat in
The henhouse the
Grapes were eyeballs
And Sue said
Jump!
She said, we
Are so beautiful
A carton of Camel
Lights later
Talent is
A blowjob
Under the table...
Skate park
Homemade halfpipe
Lost inhaler, lost sister
She said it---
Jump.
You go first...
He didn't touch
You
He once touched
Me too
Let's jump---
Look, it's like
Heaven
Cheekbone cracked
Joey if only u wur
My boyfriend
A 17 year old virgin
What's the point---
Looney Bin calling
Me home
Dark brother

Or maybe my
Lost father
In the night.

, was his name.

He was   years older than me
The party was at   house
I told the police   but they   did / did not believe me

I can / cannot testify because it was in state / out of state

I was grounded for coming home late
I was berated by my mom for losing my jacket

When I woke up, my   was on the ground

He had taken off my   and they were also on the ground
I was bleeding but did not have a tourniquet / bandage / pad /
      tampon   to use

I did / did not go to the doctor
The doctor asked me if I had been drinking / dancing / lewd /
      flirtations / skanky / promiscuous.

I did / did not answer yes / no.

He was   convicted of molesting   girls and sent to jail for   year (s).

, was his name.

Pain is Just Another Word

All this pain is icicle-white and drips
in my eyes when I stare at the sun;

I'm checking to see if God came back,
yet somehow I already know – He didn't.

Pain is another word for a drain.
Like when I watch the grey water swirl –

A mini-eddy of suds and razor stubble –
disgusting hair and flehm and spunk –

I hate it all and I am disgusted
by my humanity; it feels similar to when

The regurgitated chum of unwanted sexuality
whorled past my tongue, shaking hands with an

Acid-eaten esophagus, trailing blood like wine,
corked with only a tampon – and I am

Nauseated by my smell and myself,
but perhaps more intact in some primordial way.

It feels like the animalistic instinct
to eat one's own afterbirth; to hide

Away the scent of something he covets...
from the puma, who is coming –

His paws enormous - precise, determined.
As is my pain – of knowing I am his prey.

As are the whorls, the icicles –
so irresponsible with their tears of silver.

As is God. Lest He has forgotten
the sound of my name.

The Walking Wounded

They move along the river:
>in droves; in droves.

Their bloody stares seek
>a stranger for help;

Assistance. Amputation.
>Her shredded limb –

Which hangs – from hardly (a)
>ball joint.

No one is moving a muscle
>except for

The muscle, which swings
>in the breeze, an

Inside exposed – jaws agape
>over the shore;

Snipes even fearful
>of what they don't know – flit

From hedge
>and alight upon them.

Who, then –
>shall take this Jane Doe in?

Her wound offends you – as if was her fault
>for absorbing

The blow – the first salvo,
>in which a very many died.

Shall she be dead to you – for her fate
>of surviving;

Look at the bone exposed: in droves,
>in droves –

Not yet gone they walk the road:
        #_____ victims.

Out Here in the Void

I am out here in the void
not my bones
of course, not any meat left to speak of –
not the horrid messy muscle,
not the toothpick ossifications,
which held me together;
a scarecrow,
which scares not one single crow.

I am out here sending signals to you –
Thank you for holding me up those nights.
Thank you for laughing into my hands,
for holding my head when I hurt so bad.

I was the food one, the lack of food
won, but no one else one
ever touched me again;
never held me drowning,
never spat in my eye,
never tore my clothes, never told me
I should fuck them or die.

I am out here floating, so light like petals
and I don't fall in any wind –
and I am so light, so slight like a small child
and no one tells me that 70 lbs
is too thin. No one tells me what
to eat, or anything else for that matter.

Like we need to change your feeding tube, or we need
to give you your meds now, or it's time for your weigh in,
or it's time for group art therapy, or your family isn't coming
to see you.

Please don't feel bad that I did not make it
because I am much, so much happier without
my archaic body of bone, muscle, and heavy hair which floated like
arsenic death pools, so much of it around my face, like spaghetti.

I couldn't bear to be anything else, but a tree limb,
just limbs up, leaves open, seeing nothing – no red.

21

Just out here floating, placidly dead.
Out here, floating, but happy, and thin.

Inpatient

I think my room was No. 14
one time my pastor came

I think his name was Mark
he came to visit
I suppose to bless me
and the nurses, they asked me

May he come in

And I didn't know what to do
so I said no
he cannot
but I have wondered
all these 24 years since

Might I have succumbed to Jesus;
might I have been reborn,
maybe even saved
on the life raft that
religion has
the propensity
to relay

I would've saved all
that disgusting food
the hangovers –

All that wasted energy
from trying to kill myself
so stupidly,
so slowly.

Mark, the pastor
came to visit and
in fear of Man/God's eye
on my – body

On my sin.
I never opened the door
to let him in.

Idolescence

You always were above me. A horror movie. Freddy threw me out of the hay loft again and again – ate out my tongue. Seduced me. A young person's gullibility knows no ends. You were always prickly. Held the rights to hurt me. Thorns not enough, seems you became the male weapon to impale my body. When you touch me, it's agony. I put up with it... because no one else wants me... or accepts me. In debt for the bad decisions – the hurting of my family. I am below in the catacomb – you drop down – to have your way with me. It's only natural. Death needs to feed on something weak, yet still living – the living need to feed on something dead like your penis. Like my self respect. Rather, my regret as infinite as the spikes in your back – you extend them toward my mouth I want to bite as it rips me to pieces.

Tapping Myself in March

Ahhh it's gluttony again
This ache, this belly stab
God, such iron thorns –

Get into my wrists, worse
This new scrape of shit
I can't get all the filth off
With only my fingernails

Must cut cut cut; (I like
The way that rolls out) –
Cut me, cut me, go ahead –
Open it up

Infinite ways to release
Blood: a bud of innocent rose;
One droplet, simple trickle;
Nature's pink, morning dew

My arm awakens
My brain checks out,
The relief is worth
The vermillion color,

Forest capillaries to tap
Maple sugar's platelet run
Sweet to lick, better boiled down
In the bucket, the bath, use the cloth –

I keep it in the special spot.
I'll never run out of this...
Crucial escape
Well, if I'm smart – I hide
Inside: antagonistic cape.

Don't ask don't tell.
I swear, I wear, these
Sleeves for armors sake –
The same way I don
The crimson silk

To soothe the illness
Of my sunken brain.
To turn it off.
To feel something again –

Why I Love Owls

Do you know what it's like to be fat?
Fat is like being thrown out a car door
for not knowing how to suck cock/

Do you know what it's like to hate myself
to the core –
For being thrown out a car door for
not knowing how to suck cock/
for being fat

Do you know what it's like to try to die
from the act or non-act of eating
It's like being called fat overandoveragain and then being
thrown out a car door for not knowing how to suck cock/
and for being fat

Do you know what it's like to fail to die –
From the pathetic fail of trying to die
from the selfish act of eating and/or the selfish act of non-eating
or the act of throwing up one's insides

Like a selfish little bitch
who is a whiny piece of shit
about her stupid, wasted life –

It's like being fat. It's
Like being called a fat lez
Like wishing I was a fat lez instead...
Like failing at gagging oneself.
Like failing at gagging oneself with a disgusting cock – /

In the hopes of some kind or acceptance
by an asshole wannabe logger named Levi
who hath monikered you 'Fat-Troll'
who tells you to suck his disgusting dick/
in a Chevy S-10 with not enough Buds to ever make it
doable/tolerable

And he takes your last smoke; the one you would later need to nurse
the choke
And hepushesyou, hepushesyou:

(you: a drunk and gibbering, Fat-troll monikered, misused, mistaken, missing teen)
out of a gaping door)

"Thanks for nothing… but a fucking shitty blowjob"

Then he drives off – just like that.
And then, suddenly – you are not fat.
Neither are you cumstained.

And then you think, *is that not an owl?*
Then you think – owls don't hate fat girls –
Neither would an owl make you give them a blowjob.
Owls simply don't behave like that.

That is what it is like to be fat.
And that is also why I love owls.

Oh, I was dead at 29

doused and lit
with bikini lines
smokin' men
on my red hots
leaving them in gutters
10 in one pop.

I know what you mean
I really do

my cervical spine has fused
from looking over my shoulder
the muscles tired of
all the rubber-necking –
they done snapping back.

what did I think I would see, with
all this scouting out behind me –
Alejandro, el pendejo, flying in from Mexico?
_____ _____, with his apology
for raping me at 16?

I can only tunnel vision now
no periphery,
I'm done with #metoo
if I've no one left to tell it to –
no careers to ruin 'cept my own
with tales of the gropings
in blood clot dawns

baby mine – don't you cry
for me no more

I don't need her, I don't need
anyone

I need water, endless geysers
want to wash the grime off me

burn with sulfur any trace
of violations which occurred

on the dermatological construct
of me, daddy.
I lied. I need you.
You knew I was coming back around with this –
you know my tendency for neediness

but it is only with you I behave in this way
I don't smother any others these days –

I let them go, easily; like old
coffee spilling in the driveway

our histories dispel
as smoke

even as they pivot away from me –
I will be ok. alone is really good

alone, is what I make of it, and
death is only a month away

The prior repertoire of eating souls
is not for me anymore –
I only need you.

Light be crave
get me through
this night again, give me one
good dream that is not of
broken bottles slashing
trolls hidden in the casings
hot dogs penetrating
showers of gold teeth cascading
children lost forever and naked
predators in the woods
instead of chickadees
flitting around snatching babies
this is why my neck has fused
from the midnight run
I must have been torqued in
my hapless pillow form
till the night had passed through in
another fatal storm.

Wallet Pictures

I am going back down into a dark place; there are cobwebs like sprouts in a rotten hummus wrap; there are pictures of you from when we were happy (you had hair still, and no bitter notions) – I fell in, you swam out to save me: normal.

Sunbathing reminds me of your character choices - vain and red: a lobster-loving captain; Cain. Weinstein hooking this Virgin Writer's words and weaving them as his own eggish orb-pillows. Bloody hell / period / no pad / no advil. Immaculacy in conception were we –

Sleeping well are you? Sleeping in too? Without me there to grind the coffee with my teeth, I would think a long, undisturbed sleep suits you; while angry angry me; spiteful, jealous, pin-prick, saddle-sore arrhythmia waits –

I'm pithy. Unrefined little 'ol jaded ticked off cancer-morph, low platelet count, creamery style cholesterol and oh-my-goodness-graft; hurt me. Hurt me. Hurt me. Done yet? We done with this yet?

Small Souls

Outside my window
there is a huge raccoon
who eats live chicks
by the light of the moon
he taunts me: mean
as he plucks them clean
(ice shards for teeth)

Those chicks are my babies
it makes me weep
to think how they suffered
I don't want to talk about what I should have done
how I should have run outside
how I should have grabbed the gun
how I should have run to you
how I should have brought the gun
when you were suffering -
I was suffering too

Afraid of the toilet
the witch that lived in it
if I shit she would
stick me with a needle
so anal-retentive
I spent my young years holding the crap inside
then I grew chubby, white and blubbery
breasts swollen as rotten melons

Then I got raped,
eaten alive
by a human coon
(ice shards for teeth)
by the light of a
horrid post-dawn moon

I don't like what you're doing to me -
I whimpered
just a 16 year old virgin
on a downhill slide
to last a lifetime

Who knew I would miss all those years I shit my pants -
those were the easy ones
hell, those were the good times
cuz years get easy and flow together when the difficulty of life
courses itself in and out of your eras
when you spend it wishing for difference
for the old days - the gentle ones
not quite as hard to bear

Now all I hope for
is to live long enough
to help my children have good lives
it doesn't matter that I want to die
it's no longer about me
it's about the young children
who are scared to go to the bathroom
who are scared of the dark
who are scared of angry parents
that yell and they cower like
storm ravaged sunflowers

I am I am
the evil ogre that should get locked up
but who then would stroke
their ochre cheeks of suede
at night as they risk
the closing of their eyes
and lay there - small souls exposed
to the evil teeth of the night,
I whimper

Goodnight little ones.
Momma's here, sleep tight.

What's Eating Gilbert Grape's Mom

Heartbroken; shattered plates
aren't coming together; swelling
makes muscle plump on bone
pooling hematoma prickly blue
bruising like a comical formula

For damaged tissue, neurologic
palsy, and bloody mess elevators
arrange the bandage as a diaper
to hold the fester a little longer

In this dillapate house caving down
upon my head, my body, throbbing
with death – no chair helps me tagalong
green lawn, green lawn, before the oak
commences burning, plays dead

Smells smoke, and crackle fawn
succumbs to the obese splinter –
white wash monster consummated
her pyre comes together – over; over.

My Own Blair Witch

Here I go again, down the rabbit hole
Chasing things I cannot touch,
Wrapping their oily arms around me
Jagermeister, weed & American Spirits –
Vices I gave up years ago

God, what I wouldn't do for a cigarette
I was doing so great last night, not even crying –
Not hating myself

For being a shitty, selfish mom
For being a shitty, unloving wife
For the fucking blather in my brain

If I'm not drinking
I'm gagging myself in the bathroom
You thought I was such a lovely date
Until I puked your money down the toilet

If I'm not yo-yo dieting
I'm bingeing on spaghettios, bagels, ice cream and brownies
Even cereal, I will steal from my roommate
Coffee cake from the conference room'
Skittles from the boss' desk
I have zero pride – watch me

I eat them in a bathroom stall
I give not a shit –
Lifting up my feet if you come in
My life is over now, can anyone hear me?

One night stands with men I hated
Cocaine, beer, tequila
Curated as the many broken capillaries; as the
Forceful vomiting with Ipecac

You recommended that tactic to me
And I did it – I stole it from the drug store
Not knowing how deep I was going under

Here I go again, another spike in the climate

Hating myself violently –
It feels like a chemical surge in my chest
In my neurons it burns a little
Feels corrosive
Acid splashing on my face all the while
Oh, to be thin, even while suffering the burns

It makes me think things like:
I am a bad, bad bird

All because I had a miscreant dream
Of my son falling from a church
Balcony and then another
Having sex with my abusive step father ---

I hate everything.

My virginity taken unapologetically to
I Will be Your Father Figure –

As my hymen stained your houndstooth sheets
Put your tiny hand in mine –

I suppose you burned them or took them to a dumpster –
I will be your preacher teacher –

You wouldn't even give me your last fag –
Anything you had in mind –

Nor walk me to my Chevy Celebrity –
And I will be the one who loves you,

In the driveway, behind your mother's Caravan
till the end of time.

So fuck it – I went on a diet and made all the men love me, than shat
on their hearts. But the sad part was – I was actually shitting in my
own mouth, in my own head. All those fucks, those drinks, those
joints, those near death nights - I am still trying to bleach the brown
stains from my head, the old cum from my face –

It's a bad stain. I am a bad stain on this earth. I don't even care about
Republicans anymore –

36

it's too much to hope for good. It's too hard to get up and fight. I'm so tired, you know ---

Let my covers smother me today –
and take the light away from my eyes –
So I don't have to watch

My own Blair Witch Project
Another, stupid fucking day.

This is an Asking

Feel this -- asking; it's from the men

it's new,   like a marriage,

wants

many things   from you

red, fresh wet   things

as if you might change your name

to its name –
see,   she is whispering
see,   she must love u   sexually tempting

such as tornado damage   u r a ravaged virgin
can do to you   consonants ctrl   buckle like kn(ee)s

they said –

get up, again again   it makes you
come up for more embarrassment   harsh air

can you get up   shamedbaby
after such a pummeling   youngbride

the wind is a selfish pig
likes it rough   thinks nothing
of blowing   you down

or little pink houses ---- like bodies

around   around   around.

Antonymity

I loved you, you fucking
Idiot – didn't give a shit
For me – fat thighed baby
Diaper – filled with naive
Shit – asexual sister type –
Small, chubby cheeks
And melon breasts don't
Get teens up – long legs
Long hair, long teeth
Long tongues, long lists
Of who she laid her long
Torso down for – and for
How long – without using
Her words – short is my time
In the show – the sinister
Long life goes on
And on and on – till it
Becomes a graciously
Short lived train wreck
And shallow grave of
Jeans, training bras,
Panties and rocks, hard
Hard life worth of rocks.

Abiding the Law

Crack of my inner self
expands – persona non grata
said *drink this kill elixir*;
hapless liver, porous flab

When all she ever wanted was
to crawl back inwards

Spread wide at the legs –
make cruelest room x2
everywhere I might escape;
she is hither, and grew anew

A slice of throat
per capita allotment
this witch to dislodge
en terrorum blood clot

Which of me, would you adopt
Herr Doktor?
the halved missionary
cut down so easily –

Or the sorceress who giveth muse
to eviscerate the purgatory
for medical experiments –
to take on as your new baby

Bride of males
I could not expel –
cracked open my inner self
for Daddy's viewing pleasure

this ti
me for fod
der

i'm floating in the brine
every eye im float
ing in the formal
dyhyde – every femin
ine part of my pride
my genitals soak
ing in Cuvier's wine
my vag
ina in the curat
or's divina
tion of my kind
clit
oris in the pred
ator's mind – salted cur
ed and on disp
lay. lay
ered ed up like
appe
tizers on a plat
terred tray. but min
e, saturat
ed, wet, decomp
osing o'
er the centur
ies, mine lump
ed with animal
s in zoos, min
e treat
ed as if a differ
ent spec
ies. I am a diff
erent spec
ies that you, Cuv
ier. I am Saartjie
and my clit
oris will be com
ing around in the ne
xt life – open for
business contract

ed to wo
men only – com
ing, coming to glor
ious life – dark, jew
elled, ripe, read
y to con
sume you-----
surgic
ally conc
ise your balls, the
n hand them to the po
or enslav
ed postcolon
ials, out as Con
rad's heart for fod
der

Captive Wretch

If you care for me, eat me now. I will be safe inside your moist belly. Out here in wretched sandstorm corridor I am a number. I am a convert. They want to yell at me: Stockholm Syndrome! I answer to Esther. I answer to Mary. I am the birth of a big blue ball and called it Freedom. It's at the bottom of the ocean. Plastic bags wash up up like crabs. I go in you like an eel, slippery and fanged / I go in you parasitic to reclaim what was my birthright. What was my birthright? When the ball popped it was the waters and they drained marshes for tanneries and swamps for desalination. So - I salt the inside of you until you turn yourself to brine and melt, like a slug - shriveling in the merciless sunshine.

Leave me the fuck alone

No. Stop. I don't like what you are doing to me.
I don't want this. I am not interested. I have a boyfriend.
I'm alone. I'm married. I am HIV positive. I'm a lesbian,
I have the flu. I'm pregnant.

Leave me be. I don't want to dance. No, no drink. No
Thank you. I'm tired. I'm going home. I will call the cops.
I have a restraining order. I'm well versed in voodoo, I'm a
Witch, a heathen, a slut, a hussy, I'm full of diseases. Get the
Fuck away from me, can't you hear? I'm going to the bathroom…
into your mother's house.

No my tits aren't real. I'm underage. I'm an alien. I have two
Fake legs and a weave of animal hair. I'm a dog. A horse.
A republican. A democrat. I crashed my car into your mother's house
—

I'm homeless. I am repugnant. I'm a
Lutheran.

I'm Hitler. Imelda. Stalin. Trump.
I'm Madonna. Frida. Teresa. Hillary.

Leave me the fuck alone. Or swear to god
I'm gonna….

Coming to Terms with my Belly Snake

I saw a man pulling a deer inside-out yesterday.

I turn myself inside-out pretty often as well. In fact, I did it yesterday too: reached a tentacle down my throat, deep in the wet guts and yanked it, awful hard – came up bloody, green, scarified, guttural – then ran down the street shrieking – *stop hounding me, everybody!* Stopped for a cigarette on the curb, not caring wtf u think – hopped a bus, a freight, a jet, a Greenpeace vessel and was last seen heading under-dressed for the arctic (think monokini, flip-flops) – I once quipped: *her heart was as fleeting as the polar bears existence*; seems that was taken too serious. Earlier years: scrap-booked a life in seashells and starfish – smashed clocks with a ball-peen – chewed through thumb-drives and clipped toenails – banged to Pink Floyd and belted opera to Nirvana – Fantasia, trippin' on shrooms – under black light back in '92. Later years: slow crawl in a woman's larynx, uninvited, I give chase - *stop scaring the others!* – all the happy, blithe, ant-hill people. This destruction is only meant to be therapeutic for the walking wounded, the initiated... Now: *why do you keep fighting,* she asks me. I reply, *I hold due the tragedy of imagining, and I am too scared to surrender.*

I am a Yoyo

I am a yoyo –
I know how to walk the dog.
Roll him alongside – he heels like a servant;
my tools take hold – I am your alpha bitch, baby.

I am a yoyo –
I can be like Yoko and love John;
I can survive and be a widow when he's gone –
spreading my message of peace and love,
despite the cauldron of hate we sip from.

I am a yoyo –
I can suck you off like a dam unleashed
your ire released.
I am a damsel in distress,
gloves, garter, anything you want - you got it.

I am a yoyo –
I like women
but I married a man.
I like children, but prefer growing old
to my teenage years.

I am a yoyo –
You can hold me tightly to you
but I'm like the dove
I'll always fly away –

As soon as you release me
never knowing where the hell my nest might be.

I am a yoyo –
You will never see me cry
You will never see me cry, cuz boyz don't cry
But girls do and I am a girl and if beaten,
My tears are real saltwater.

– Either gender –

It's true,
you *brute* you.

I am a yoyo –
You do not do, Daddy,
yet I will keep snapping back up to you –

An accordion blind,
a wrinkle in time –

When you flick your wrist,
a talisman
landing safely in your hand –

Only to be shot out again
at your whimsy –
down the leg of
your slim jimmy –

To be walked like a dog
crank the merciless cog.

Loving and hating you
all this whiling away of this hardest time.

The Hunters are Coming

I hate November.
My stomach is in knots
and I'm glancing over my shoulder –
I'm irritable and worried like when
the madman tags along in my dreams
cackling cruelly as I fall
from the tops of buildings like rag-dolls;
him, on his hands and knees
as we scavenge through the leaves for
my lost teeth.

The Hunters are coming.
They are putting on their camo,
they are coming out of their campers,
they are cleaning the butts and phalluses of their flesh weapons
and the cock mechanisms of their metallic weapons –

They are coming for me. They are coming for you.
The other prey and I
no longer know where to run.
We are bumping into trees and
into each other
looking for boulders large enough to cover our asses –
looking for a blind of our own to keep us blind from
the night vision goggles
that see through my dress,

And the date rape
bait feed that
lures me closer –

Easy to pull my pants down so they may
hunt what they like, licking their chops
they've eaten me again and again,
every year the same feast.

My corpse is in the smoker house
making jerky of my thighs.
They have stacked enough wood
to transform me into venison, steaks, stew, casseroles –

And I am only one of the many faces
that will hang on the walls this year;
if you go there after
hunting, to have a beer with your
hunting friends,
Look into my eyes, because even though my
head is stuffed with…cotton and formaldehyde
they could not remove the anger in my eye as
those are not orbs of glass
but my real eyes still –

I tricked them into keeping them there
wasn't that smart of me?
They shot me through the heart
and in my lungs
and in my ass –

Too bad
it did so much damage to my body –
less meat for them to enjoy
but hey, they didn't shoot my head open
with their virile balls of fire.

Of course not, as they wanted it on the living room wall
as a testament to their prowess –
a tally of testosterone
a trophy – someone's trophy.

Little did they know it sparked a fire in my eye –
they won't be able to enjoy their afternoon beer
as I will be staring them down,
singeing their red beards to ash –

No longer afraid of their man weapons
they've already had what they wanted of me –
so look out: I'm eating men's hair *like air*.
I take what I need, want –
give them bad dreams of a madwoman: me

My body of a woman
with the head of a doe
and snakes for my hair,
snacking on men; cracking open

their vessels like coconuts
in hurricanes of estrogen –

My vagina open, gaping,
looking them in the eye
peeking over their shoulder,
laughing orgasmically
as they look through the leaves
for their buckshot, their slugs, their dragon's breath
that fell out of their mouth, gums hung like rubies
the ones they ate me with –
now a smattering of spent metal.

The Hunters are coming.
For me, for you.
I'm too tired to run
and they dismantled my blind to hide behind.

I think this year
I'll just lay down in a field –
the combine has already eaten my friend, the corn.
I'm so scared,
I'm so tired.

Next year I'll be a brave deer.
I hate November.

How I Wish Not to Own This

I'm going dark on this one baby.
I'm restricting calories
like when I was a virgin
and you told everyone (they should)
fuck me.

I used to dance on tables at parties
my reputation of inexperience –
famous for tempting gyrations; 17 yr old twerk

Like Madonna – bridal
young and disconnected
white and virginal, laughed at – disrespected.

Falling off that table never
hurt so bad as the real thing –
abyss bound and throat gagging

*

blood flowers grow in swamps
in pitch dark madness
in caves in nooks and crannies
flowing out of the ground
hymen tsunami

when the necklace broke
gold waterfall of innocence
fluttering down like maple
tree spinners and my face frozen in
time forever

broken smile cocked sideways
incredulous – like
a crack starts in the ground
and then becomes an
earthquake
swallows itself

and all the pretty jewelry from
grampa inscribed so tenderly

Lizza – *she* gets eaten up whole
by the entire cadre of dirt rocks
and sandmen.

Blood finds a way always downhill
just ask a dying soldier on a hillside
they'll tell you – women will also tell you – stay uphill
tampons are only as good as where you
put them, like friends –

Scarlet flowers flow
the heart fistula grows
this can't be my life.

*

I didn't ask for this. So –
please be kind to the youth;
just let her(me) be. Not have me become quite
this damaged –
Please.

The Taste of Men

little do I know of aging and fragility –
it's not the twiglike bones
creaking with fortysomething,
which bother me

it's the taste of men in my
mouth from my teens and twenties
(but not like it sounds) – the feel

of my head in a vice and a squeeze
so implied the esophagus pops out,
like a glass eye –

until I slip and drown in
a cocaine hottub;
I wake and I am naked.
The party has ended –

some say glass tastes of nothing –
but I say it must – if it's made of sand –
grit n grains in everything I eat; I drink –
ginger ale grinds new gizzard meat

glitterati, we gettin' scissored
was my boytoy beat
and the slivers came and went
made jagged scars –
the ones I now curate

never leave the egg salad;
salt and peppered like my hair now –
tupperware like an isolation cage –
mustard & mayo; wrinkle cream... support hose

there was even fiberglass in
the Marlboro Lights –
and the taste of those is still...

ruby blood upon my mouth,
forceful sex within my throat –
and I flick back and forth this many-layered

tongue – a film of slime for every man I...

with soap and washcloth in hand;
a toothbrush works between the lips –
every woman I meet nowadays
learns how to clean her mouth up.

Like Clockwork

In the dark,

All silence is a taunting bloom
it mocks me with its incessant aplomb

It is that one of cruel deformity
one who tickles my discomfort with civility

Not this man not this man
not these fingers of

Madness – a raucous chuckle
clockwork orange; a test debacle

In a bedroom, with eyes sewn up, knives
become my fingers and lips, blindfolded

Not so dark not so dark
not so fooled blindly –

Dangerous as the slicing realm, it returns
when night is done being night, and

There you are again upright, smiling at me---
endless ways to describe the hurt; in the day

Not my body not my body
you touched my

Body; lying prone & accursed
They like to say – that all that matters is that

The sun rose & chased down the greasy sky
& drove away the sealing wax of coffin pine

I still tend to say – not this light not this light
Not shining… so brightly… today.

I want a gun

I wanna be Daisy Duke
Skinny legs and apple-round the rest of me
I wanna be Lynda Carter
pit you against my truth lasso
Be Jewel; kiss crooked-tooth
Jewel; be a folk singer
be adorable.
In the subway panhandling the coins
knowing I get paid in pennies
for doing what I love –
Kicking Lex Luthor's ass
Fucking Hal and Flash,
pitting them against each other
and the devil in my brass tits.
I wanna be Dolly Parton, skinny legs
Shock and Awe
apple-round the rest of me
Islands in the stream –
O Kenny darlin'
What we are is Boss Hog Bait.
I wanna be cutoff shorts n corsets
I want a gun.

Go ahead – kick this hornet's nest

I don't want to play anymore –
no sunshine day charades.

I don't want to be a good girl –
no pigtails, barrettes or braids.

I want to shave my skull clean, be it cancer-morph; or punk:
Lisbeth, I said, is my name to you –

No bim-boms, perms or highlights...
Bring not some solicitor's rape kit.

I want it to glare in the sun, atomic –
no little woman here, folks.

As an Old Woman – Satisfied

Life for this discrepancy treaty – in theory:
Make a change – tear the misfit apart
Build a cantilevered teen fort which props her
Up. Blair Witch death & panicking; pretending
Above ground – under sky. Nothing here is
Unthinkable. Cept dirt. Cept sin. Cept some
Proper joyous beginnings. Proper Sex
Positionings. Not jammed into a couch.

Head cocked sidewards; neck broke, akimbo
Baby. Sixteen. Legs out, splayed. Highway paint;
Drying tire track shapes. V-shape honing towards
A freight train fate. Mistook. Mistake. Took what
Was not take-able. Not able to talk about this
Anymore. Not proper for Mum's dinner table.

Easier in the oaken hideaway where words
Lift me up, then become balloons – float me
Away, away from the torn jeans, simple discarded
Teen – Above Good Parson's burial ground; under
God's care: a heavenly sky-fall. Shall she not ask,
Why? Ask: for what reason other than her grow
Season abounding. Never allow the other way
Around – reliving out any more such things, until,
As an old woman, satisfied – I die.

Acknowledgements

Thank you to all the survivors who give me the strength to write this and hold me up; I hold you up.

Thank you to Amanda and Beth at Femme Salvé Books for breathing life into this book once more.

Thank you to my family for not giving up on me.

With love,

Eli

Prior Publications

Thank you gentle editors for taking a chance on my work. eh

Was it Rape and Doing Nothing at a Party (While a Drunk Girl Gets Destroyed By a Sex Predator), *Milk & Beans,* April, 2018
Sue's Death Wish, Why I Love Owls, *Anti-Heroin Chic,* July, 2018
Pain is Just Another Word, The Walking Wounded, *Dwarts Magazine,* Spring, 2018
Tapping Myself in March, *Rising Phoenix Review,* 2018
Oh, I was dead at 29, *Bone & Ink Press,* 2018
Small Souls, *The Mad River,* May, 2018
Idolescense, Wallet Pictures, Coming to Terms with my Belly Snake, Captive Wretch, *Former Cactus,* 2018
How I Wish Not to Own This, *Red Fez,* 2017
I Am a Yo-Yo, *Quail Bell,* 2018
The Hunters are Coming, *The Woman, Inc.,* 2018
As An Old Woman - Satisfied, Pensacola Girls, *Bone & Ink Press,* 2018
I Want a Gun, *Occulum,* 2017
Go ahead - kick this hornet's nest, *Moonchild Magazine,* Issue 3

About the Author

Elisabeth Horan is an imperfect creature from Vermont advocating for animals, children and those suffering alone and in pain – especially those ostracized by disability and mental illness. She is Editor in Chief at Animal Heart Press. She has several chaps and collections including *Bad Mommy / Stay Mommy* at Fly on the Wall Press, *Just to the Right of the Stove* at Twist In Time Press, and *Self-Portrait* from Cephalo Press. She is a poetry mentor and proud momma to Peter and Thomas.

She recently earned her MFA from Lindenwood University and received a 2018 Best of the Net Nomination from *Midnight Lane Boutique* and a 2018 Pushcart Nomination from *Cease Cows*.

Follow her @ehoranpoet and ehoranpoet.net

www.ingramcontent.com/pod-product-compliance
Lightning Source LLC
Chambersburg PA
CBHW071953100426
42736CB00043B/3188